Granola Bar Recipes
Delicious Recipes For Holiday

Copyright © 2021

All rights reserved.

DEDICATION

The author and publisher have provided this e-book to you for your personal use only. You may not make this e-book publicly available in any way. Copyright infringement is against the law. If you believe the copy of this e-book you are reading infringes on the author's copyright, please notify the publisher at: https://us.macmillan.com/piracy

Contents

Oatmeal Raisin Granola Bars Recipe 1
No-Bake Granola Bars 14
Dark Chocolate Peanut Butter Energy Bars 26
Acrobatic Granola Bars 29
Nut Free Crunchy Granola Bars 33
Chewy No Bake Granola Bars 36
Chewy Raspberry Apple Granola Bars 38
Skinny Funfetti Cake Batter Granola Bars 41
Healthy Apple Pie Granola Bar Bites 44
Healthy Chocolate Chip Granola Bar Bites 46
Homemade Granola Bars – the Winning Recipe 50
Healthy No-bake Granola Bars 57

Oatmeal Raisin Granola Bars Recipe

Last weekend, my family and I fell in love with making our own homemade granola bars. We made Trail Mix Granola Bars and Peanut Butter S'more Granola Bars. They are super simple and taste delicious. They are so easy that my 7 yr old can make them by himself, and he did! Today he wanted to make them to take for the after game snack for his baseball team. We ended up making two versions - a straight S'more version (like the Peanut Butter S'more Granola Bars, but with no peanut butter - there are kids with nut allergies on the team.) The second version was my son's creation - an oatmeal raisin granola bar with cinnamon. He did everything by himself, except the pouring of the hot syrup into the mixing bowl. He was so proud! He told all his team mates that he made the granola bars, and repeatedly asked them how they like the snack. Adorable!

Needless to say, everyone loved them and everyone was thoroughly impressed.

This is how he made his cinnamon oatmeal raisin bars:

He put 1 3/4 cups of oats, 1 cup of puffed rice cereal and 1/2 cup of raisins in a large mixing bowl. - We are using the same bowl that we just made the S'more version in, so please disregard the chocolate on the bowl. Saving dishes is always a priority. :)

He then put 1/2 stick of butter, 1/4 cup honey and 1/3 cup of dark brown sugar in a pot on the stove. Turned the heat to medium and stirred the ingredients together.

When the mixture started to bubble, he watched the clock for 2 minutes and then turned the stove off.

It was at this point (when he was waiting his 2 minutes for the syrup to be done) that he asked if we could add cinnamon sugar to the mixture. I told him that we didn't need any more sugar, because of the honey and brown sugar in the syrup but that cinnamon would be OK. We sprinkled enough to cover the top (probably about 1/4 tsp), and then mixed it all in.

I poured on the hot syrup and he started mixing.

When everything was completely covered in syrup, my boy wanted to add some chocolate chips. (Of course, I mentioned before that chocolate is pretty much a standard in our house.) This is completely optional. We added 1/3 cup.

As soon as the chocolate was mixed in, I dumped it into a 9x9 pan and started to flatten it out. My handsome man did most of this, but I just happened to take the shot with my hand in the picture.

You really want to make sure to press down hard, so that everything gets good and stuck together. Now , our hands are covered in melted chocolate so we washed our hands and put the granola bars in the fridge to cool for at least 30 minutes.

When they were cool, I turned them out onto a cutting board.

I cup them into 7 long strips,

and then cut the strips in half - 14 bars. There are 14 members of his baseball team. Isn't it wonderful when things work out?

From here we just put each granola bar in a zip-top baggie with a S'more granola bar, so that each child word have their pre-portioned snack. Served along side a 100% juice pack and it was an awesome and nutritious snack! (The hubby and I hate it when parents bring junk food for the team snack. -Stepping on my soap box. We should be giving our kids healthy snacks and treats. We want them to be healthy and grow up the best they can. Our kids will only act as good as the food we put in them. Just think about that for a second. Our kids have been given candy and doughnuts for an after game snack on more than one occasion. Really people? Just sayin'. OK stepping down off of my soap box.)

No-Bake Granola Bars

These chewy no-bake granola bars are really easy to make and so delicious that every time I make some, half the pan is gone before I can put them away! I started doubling the recipe so I would have enough to set aside for snacks for the week! The great thing about this recipe is that you probably have the basic ingredients in your pantry already AND you can literally put these together in under 5 minutes! Plus they have no preservatives!

Chewy No-Bake Granola Bars - These are so good! No preservatives and you probably have all the ingredients in your pantry already!

Disclosure: This post may contain affiliate links to Amazon and/or Etsy, which means that I may earn a small commission from some of the links in this post. Please see our Disclosure Page for more information.

This time I made white chocolate coconut cranberry bars but you can top them with whatever you like – mini chocolate chips, sliced almonds, chopped dried fruit, pecans, butterscotch chips, mini marshmallows, seeds…whatever! I've been making these for years but the recipe originally came from Lauren's Lately (and she adapted it from Rachel Ray).

No-Bake Granola Bars

Ingredients needed to make no-bake granola bar can be found in your pantry.

INGREDIENTS:

2 cups quick cooking oats (not rolled oats)

1 cup rice crispy cereal

1/4 cup butter (real butter)

1/4 cup honey

1/4 cup packed brown sugar

1/2 teaspoon vanilla

1/3 cup shredded coconut (optional)

Toppings of your choice (mine are craisins and white chocolate chips)

DIRECTIONS:

1. In a large bowl, stir oats, rice cereal and shredded coconut (optional) together. Set this aside

2. In a small pot – melt butter, brown sugar and honey over medium high heat. Stir and let it start to bubble.

These chewy no-bake granola bars are really easy to make and so delicious that every time I make some, half the pan is gone before I can put them away! I started doubling the recipe so I would have enough to set aside for snacks for the week! The great thing about this recipe is that you probably have the basic ingredients in your pantry already AND you can literally put these together in under 5 minutes! Plus they have no preservatives!

Chewy No-Bake Granola Bars - These are so good! No preservatives and you probably have all the ingredients in your pantry already!

Disclosure: This post may contain affiliate links to Amazon and/or Etsy, which means that I may earn a small commission from some of the links in this post. Please see our Disclosure Page for more information.

This time I made white chocolate coconut cranberry bars but you can top them with whatever you like – mini chocolate chips, sliced almonds, chopped dried fruit, pecans, butterscotch chips, mini marshmallows, seeds…whatever! I've been making these for years but the recipe originally came from Lauren's Lately (and she adapted it from Rachel Ray).

No-Bake Granola Bars

Ingredients needed to make no-bake granola bar can be found in your pantry.

INGREDIENTS:

2 cups quick cooking oats (not rolled oats)

1 cup rice crispy cereal

1/4 cup butter (real butter)

1/4 cup honey

1/4 cup packed brown sugar

1/2 teaspoon vanilla

1/3 cup shredded coconut (optional)

Toppings of your choice (mine are craisins and white chocolate chips)

DIRECTIONS:

1. In a large bowl, stir oats, rice cereal and shredded coconut (optional) together. Set this aside

2. In a small pot – melt butter, brown sugar and honey over medium high heat. Stir and let it start to bubble.

3. Once it it starts boiling, reduce the heat and cook for 2 minutes stirring. remove from heat

4. Add the vanilla and stir

5. Pour over dry ingredients and mix well until everything is completely coated.

6. At this point you can add in your mix-in items if you like your bars that way (I put mine on top). Just be sure that the mixture is a bit on the cool side if adding chocolate chips otherwise they will melt.

7. Pour into a well greased 13×9 baking dish (if you like thicker bars you can double the recipe or use a smaller pan). Spread out your mixture to fit the pan and sprinkle on any toppings (I like mine on top instead of mixed in)

Super Easy No-Bake Granola Bars

By Manuela Williams

These chewy no-bake granola bars are really easy to make and so delicious that every time I make some, half the pan is gone before I can put them away! I started doubling the recipe so I would have enough to set aside for snacks for the week! The great thing about this recipe is that you probably have the basic ingredients in your pantry already AND you can literally put these together in under 5 minutes! Plus they have no preservatives!

Chewy No-Bake Granola Bars - These are so good! No preservatives and you probably have all the ingredients in your pantry already!

Disclosure: This post may contain affiliate links to Amazon and/or Etsy, which means that I may earn a small commission from some of the links in this post. Please see our Disclosure Page for more information.

This time I made white chocolate coconut cranberry bars but you can top them with whatever you like – mini chocolate chips, sliced almonds, chopped dried fruit, pecans, butterscotch chips, mini marshmallows, seeds…whatever! I've been making these for years but the recipe originally came from Lauren's Lately (and she adapted it from Rachel Ray).

No-Bake Granola Bars

Ingredients needed to make no-bake granola bar can be found in your pantry.

INGREDIENTS:

2 cups quick cooking oats (not rolled oats)

1 cup rice crispy cereal

1/4 cup butter (real butter)

1/4 cup honey

1/4 cup packed brown sugar

1/2 teaspoon vanilla

1/3 cup shredded coconut (optional)

Toppings of your choice (mine are craisins and white chocolate chips)

DIRECTIONS:

1. In a large bowl, stir oats, rice cereal and shredded coconut (optional) together. Set this aside

2. In a small pot – melt butter, brown sugar and honey over medium high heat. Stir and let it start to bubble.

3. Once it it starts boiling, reduce the heat and cook for 2 minutes stirring. remove from heat

4. Add the vanilla and stir

How to make no bake granola bars

5. Pour over dry ingredients and mix well until everything is completely coated.

6. At this point you can add in your mix-in items if you like your bars that way (I put mine on top). Just be sure that the mixture is a bit on the cool side if adding chocolate chips otherwise they will melt.

7. Pour into a well greased 13×9 baking dish (if you like thicker bars you can double the recipe or use a smaller pan). Spread out your mixture to fit the pan and sprinkle on any toppings (I like mine on top instead of mixed in)

how to make no-bake granola bars. They're super easy to make and you probably have all the ingredients in your pantry.

8. Press very firmly. I wet my hands with cold water and press down hard all around the pan. If you do not press firmly your bars will not hold together.

9. Place the pan into the fridge for 20-25 minutes then cut into whatever size bars you like.

DARK CHOCOLATE PEANUT BUTTER ENERGY BARS

SERVES: 10

CUISINE: American

CATEGORY: Snacks

PREP TIME: 10 mins COOK TIME: 5 mins TOTAL TIME: 15 mins

INGREDIENTS:

1 teaspoon vanilla

1/4 cup raw honey

1/2 cup natural unsweetened peanut butter (or almond butter)

2 tablespoons coconut oil

1/2 cup raw almonds

1/2 cup raw walnuts

1/2 cup raw pecans

1/2 cup raw cashews

5 medjool dates

1/4 cup sunflower seeds

1/4 cup shredded coconut, unsweetened

1/4 cup 80% cacao dark chocolate chips (omit for SCD)

INSTRUCTIONS:

Combine the vanilla, honey, peanut butter, and coconut oil in a saucepan over medium-low heat.

While the mixture is heating, place all of the nuts and dates in a food processor and chop until the mixture resembles course sand.

Add the shredded coconut and sunflower seeds and pulse a few times until the sunflower seeds are roughly chopped.

Remove the coconut oil mixture from the stove once it has melted, then stir in the nut mixture.

Line an 8×8 baking pan with parchment paper, then pour the granola bar mixture into the pan.

Place another piece of parchment on top, and use your palms to press the mixture into the pan evenly. Make sure to pack it down as tightly as possible. This will help the bars bind and not crumble. Sprinkle the chocolate chips on top and press them in lightly.

Place in the freezer to set for 2 hours. Lift the parchment paper out of the pan and place on a cutting board. Use a sharp knife to cut the bars into rectangles.

You can store these in the refrigerator for 2 weeks, or the freezer for a few months. If storing in the freezer, remove the bars for about 20 minutes prior to serving.

Acrobatic Granola Bars

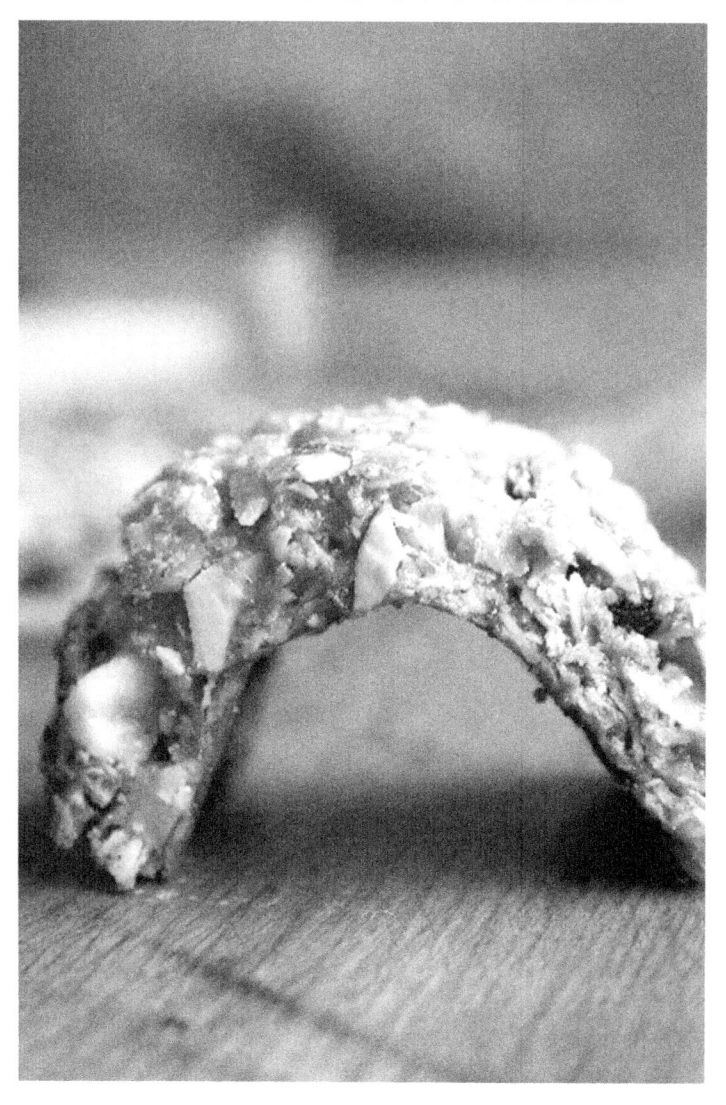

INGREDIENTS

GRANOLA BAR MIX:

4 cups rolled oats

2 cups sliced almonds

2 cups sweetened coconut

GRANOLA BARS:

1/4 cup unsalted butter, melted

6 tablespoons brown sugar (1/4 cup + 2 tablespoons)

1/3 cup almond butter or peanut butter (I prefer almond butter. PB definitely dominates.)

1/4 cup corn syrup (or honey, just know that the honey might not provide as chewy a texture as you might like)

1 teaspoon vanilla extract

2 cups of the above mix (or use 1 cup of rolled oats + 1/2 cup slivered almonds + 1/2 cup sweetened coconut)

3 tablespoons wheat germ (toasted or untoasted)

3/4 or 1 teaspoon kosher salt (I use 1 teaspoon, but if you are sensitive to salt, perhaps start with 3/4)

1/2 cup chopped cashews* (I used toasted and unsalted)

1/4 cup dried fruit**

* Almonds, walnuts, hazelnuts, pistachios — pick your favorite** In the photos, I used dried blueberries, which I thought I was going to love, but which I found to be a little too overpowering. I prefer dried cranberries and raisins, but imagine cherries, apricots, dates and figs would work nicely, too.

INSTRUCTIONS

FOR THE MIX:

Combine all in a bowl. Place in a ziplock bag until ready to make the granola bars. (As noted above, this bag will yield 4 batches of granola bars.)

FOR THE BARS:

Preheat oven to 350°F. Lay a piece of parchment paper over a 9×9-inch baking pan so that it will cover the bottom as well as the sides of the pan. Press the paper into the pan to line it. (If you can secure the parchment paper to the pan with clips, it will help when you are spreading the batter into the pan.)

Melt the butter (if you haven't already), then add it to a small mixing bowl along with the brown sugar, butter, corn syrup and vanilla.

In a large mixing bowl, add the granola bar mix (or the noted smaller quantities of oats, almonds and coconut) along with the wheat germ, salt, cashews and dried fruit. Toss with your hands to combine. UPDATE: I just made a batch this morning (7-17-2012), and this time I pulsed all of these dried ingredients (cashews and dried cranberries included) in the food processor. I like the texture of the baked bar when the ingredients have been pulsed briefly. It's your call. You lose a bit of the chunky texture, so if you like that, maybe try one batch with the dry ingredients pulsed and another batch with them not pulsed. Also, you don't want to purée the ingredients so that they start clumping together. The nuts and dried berries should still be in coarse pieces. (See photo below.)

Add the wet ingredients to the dry ingredients and mix with a spatula until nicely combined. Spread into prepared pan and flatten. Bake for 20 to 25 minutes or until lightly browned on top. (The longer you bake it, the firmer the final bar will be. It might take a batch or two for you to realize what texture you prefer.) Remove from oven and let cool on rack for 25 minutes. Pull up on the parchment paper and remove the block from the pan. Lay it on a cutting board and cut the bar into pieces. Let cool completely before storing.

Nut Free Crunchy Granola Bars

Serves: 12

Ingredients

2 ½ cups old fashioned rolled oats (not quick or instant)

½ cup maple syrup

½ tsp salt

¼ cup canola oil

1 cup sunflower seeds

½ cup dried mixed berries

½ cup sweetened coconut flakes

Instructions

Preheat oven to 325 degrees F or 163 degrees C. Line a baking pan with parchment paper.

In a small saucepan over medium heat, combine maple syrup, salt and canola oil. Heat until a it becomes a thin liquid, which means it will come off the spoon quickly when you pull it up from the pan.

In a magic bullet or food processor, place ½ cup of the oats and pulse to a flour consistency.

To a bowl add the ground up oats and the 2 cups of oats that were not ground up, sunflower seeds, mixed berries, and coconut. Add maple syrup and oil mixture.

Using a large wooden spoon combine all the ingredients well. Pour into pan and smash down evenly into the prepared pan. Bake for 23-25 minutes.

Allow granola bars to cool completely in the pan.

Take out of pan when cool and cut into 12 pieces. These granola bars are crunchy so when you cut them into pieces there will be bits that break off and you will have a small bowl of granola left for sprinkling. Place granola and bars in an air tight container.

Chewy No Bake Granola Bars

4 tablespoons (1/2 stick) unsalted butter

1/2 cup packed light brown sugar (I used Sucanat)

1/4 cup honey

2-1/2 cups oats or leftover granola

1/2 cup total of the following ingredients: wheat germ {about 1/4 cup}, ground flax seeds {about 2 tablespoons} and whole flax seeds {about 2 tablespoons}. Or substitute with more oatmeal, rice cereal, or nuts.

1/2 cup Craisins

1/2 cup chopped almonds (I used sunflower seeds)

1/2 cup semisweet chocolate chips (didn't use, I was out)

*I added 2 Tbls Chia seeds

In a medium saucepan, combine the brown sugar with the honey and butter. Bring the mixture to a boil over medium-high heat, then lower the heat to medium-low and simmer until the sugar dissolves, about 2 minutes. Remove the saucepan from the heat.

Add the remaining ingredients, except for the chocolate chips, to the saucepan and fold the ingredients to evenly coat with the sauce. Transfer the granola mixture to a 9-by-13-inch ungreased baking pan and press firmly to evenly fill. Gently press the chocolate chips onto the top of the granola. Let the granola mixture set in the fridge until firm, about 15 minutes, then cut into 2-1/4-by 3-inch bars.

Store in the fridge.

Chewy Raspberry Apple Granola Bars

These wholesome snack bars are so easy to make and full of bright fruit flavors. They're a great healthy option for breakfast, snacks, or even dessert!

1 tsp coconut oil, melted

½ cup (120g) unsweetened applesauce, room temperature

⅓ cup (80mL) skim milk

1 tbsp (15mL) honey

1 tsp ground cinnamon

2 ½ cups (250g) old-fashioned oats (measured like this and gluten-free, if necessary)

1 cup (140g) frozen unsweetened raspberries, diced

Preheat the oven to 350°F, and lightly coat an 8"-square baking pan with nonstick cooking spray.

In a large bowl, stir together the oil and applesauce until smooth. Mix in the milk, honey and cinnamon until thoroughly combined. Stir in the oats until evenly coated with the applesauce mixture. Gently fold in the raspberries.

Press the oat mixture into the prepared pan, and bake at 350°F for 16-19 minutes. Cool completely to room temperature in the pan before slicing into 10 bars.

Notes: For a vegan version, substitute your favorite non-dairy milk and agave in place of the honey.

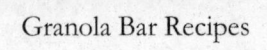

It's important for the applesauce to be at room temperature to prevent the melted coconut oil from re-solidifying.

For best storage results, tightly wrap each individual bar in plastic wrap and store in the refrigerator until ready to eat.

Skinny Funfetti Cake Batter Granola Bars

These healthy granola bars taste like your favorite childhood cupcake flavor! With their buttery flavor and bright rainbow sprinkles, these bars will disappear really quickly at snack time. Store any leftovers in an airtight container or tightly sealed inside plastic wrap.

1 tsp coconut oil, melted

½ c unsweetened applesauce

1/3 c skim milk

1 tbsp honey

1 ½ tsp butter extract

2 ½ c old-fashioned oats

3 tbsp rainbow jimmies (the long, thin sprinkles)

Preheat the oven to 300°F, and lightly coat an 8"-square baking pan with nonstick cooking spray.

In a large bowl, stir together the coconut oil, applesauce, milk, honey, and butter extract until smooth. Add in the oats, stirring until thoroughly coated. Fold in the jimmies.

Gently press the mixture into the prepared pan, and bake at 300°F for 13-16 minutes, or until the center is no longer wet to the touch. Cool completely to room temperature in the pan before slicing into bars.

Notes: Vegetable oil, canola oil, or melted butter may be substituted in place of the coconut oil.

Any milk (2%, 1%, whole, or non-dairy) may be substituted in place of the skim milk.

Agave, brown sugar, or granulated sugar may be substituted in place of the honey.

Healthy Apple Pie Granola Bar Bites

These healthy snacks taste just like the iconic dessert! They'll keep for at least 6 days if stored in an airtight container in the refrigerator.

1 ½ cups (45g) crisp brown rice cereal

1 cup (100g) old-fashioned oats (measured like this and gluten-free if necessary)

1 ½ tsp ground cinnamon

1 tsp coconut oil or unsalted butter, melted

½ cup (126g) unsweetened applesauce, room temperature

¼ cup (60g) plain nonfat Greek yogurt

2 tbsp (30mL) honey

½ tsp salt

½ cup (60g) finely diced apple

Preheat the oven to 300°F, and lightly coat an 8"-square pan with nonstick cooking spray.

In a medium bowl, combine the rice cereal, oats, and cinnamon. In a separate bowl, stir together the coconut oil and applesauce. Add in the Greek yogurt, honey, and salt, mixing until thoroughly combined. Stir in the cereal mixture. Gently fold in the diced apple.

Gently press the mixture into the prepared pan. Bake at 300°F for 14-17 minutes or until light golden and the center feels firm to the touch. Cool completely to room temperature in the pan before slicing into squares.

Notes: Regular crisp rice cereal may be substituted for the brown rice cereal.

Healthy Chocolate Chip Granola Bar Bites

These healthy snacks are perfect for any chocoholic! They're hearty, chewy, and absolutely full of chocolate. They'll keep for at least a week if stored in an airtight container in the refrigerator.

1 tsp coconut oil, melted

2 large egg whites, room temperature

¼ cup (60g) plain nonfat Greek yogurt, room temperature

3 tbsp (45mL) honey

½ tsp salt

1 ½ cups (45g) crisp brown rice cereal

1 cup (100g) old-fashioned oats (measured like this and gluten-free if necessary)

2 ½ tbsp (35g) miniature chocolate chips, divided

Preheat the oven to 300°F, and lightly coat an 8"-square pan with nonstick cooking spray.

In a medium bowl, whisk together the coconut oil and egg whites. Add in the Greek yogurt, honey, and salt, stirring after each addition until thoroughly incorporated. Stir in the rice cereal and oats. Gently fold in 2 tablespoons of miniature chocolate chips.

Gently press the mixture into the prepared pan using a spatula, and gently press the remaining chocolate chips into the top. Bake at 300°F for 16-19 minutes or until light golden and the center feels firm to the touch. Cool completely to room temperature in the pan before slicing into squares.

Notes: Regular crisp rice cereal may be substituted for the brown rice cereal. In a pinch, lightly crushed rice pocket cereal may also be substituted.

Unsalted butter or any other oil may be substituted for the coconut oil.

Pure maple syrup or agave may be substituted for the honey.

I do not recommend substituting regular-sized chocolate chips. Their bigger size may cause the granola bar bites to fall apart.

Homemade Granola Bars – the Winning Recipe

Ingredients:

Granola Bar Recipes

1/2 c. honey or corn syrup {I used 1/4 c. of each}

1/2 c. brown sugar

1/2 c. peanut butter

2 c. quick oats

2 c. Rice Krispy cereal

1/4 c. ground flax seed

1 or 2 T. wheat germ {optional — and I did not add this}

1 c. total of your favorite mix-ins {I used chocolate chips, but you could also mix and match dried fruit, nuts, seeds, etc.}

Directions:

In a small sauce pan, mix honey {or corn syrup} and brown sugar.

Cook over medium-high heat until sugar is completely dissolved — stirring constantly.

Remove from heat and quickly stir in peanut butter.

Mix the oats, cereal, flax seed, and optional wheat germ in a large bowl.

Pour honey mixture over dry ingredients — mix well.

Stir in chocolate chips, nuts, fruit, and any other "mix-ins"

Press mixture into a 9" x 13" pan that has been greased or lined with wax paper. {I find it works best when I put another piece of wax paper on top of the bars and press down with a measuring cup.}

Granola Bar Recipes

Let cool and "firm up" — kind of like Rice Krispy Bars

Cut into bars and store in an air-tight container. I cut mine into 24 bars that were about 1" x 4" {8 rows by 3 rows}. I used a pastry cutter/scraper because it cuts really straight lines — but a long knife would work just fine too.

And since I used chocolate chips, I figured it would be best to store our granola bars in the refrigerator so they don't melt!

HEALTHY NO-BAKE GRANOLA BARS

INGREDIENTS

75 grams (1/2 cup) raw almonds roughly chopped

150 grams (1 1/2 cup) rolled oats or gluten free rolled oat

2 tablespoons flax seeds

2 tablespoons mixed seeds or sunflower seeds

140 grams (1 cup) medjool dates pitted

2 tablespoons chia seeds

75 grams (1/4 cup) agave nectar or honey for no-vegan

60 grams (1/4 cup) creamy peanut butter

60 grams (1/2 cup) dried cranberries

INSTRUCTIONS

Preheat the oven to 180 degrees C (350 degrees F).

Line a 20x20 cm (8x8 inches) baking pan with aluminum foil or parchment paper, leaving the foil to extend up the sides. This will make it easier to remove the granola bars from the pan. Brush lightly with oil to prevent sticking.

In a food processor, coarsely chop the almonds.

Spread the rolled oats, chopped almonds, mixed seeds and flax seeds on a baking tray and toast them for 10 minutes, until they are slightly golden.

Transfer to a large bowl.

Process the dates in a food processor until they become a ball.

Add the crushed dates and chia seeds to the oats mixture.

In a small saucepan over low heat, warm the agave nectar and peanut butter until runny.

Pour over the dry mixture and mix well until everything is evenly coated and the dates are disperse throughout.

Transfer the mixture to the baking pan and press down with a spatula or with your wet hands.

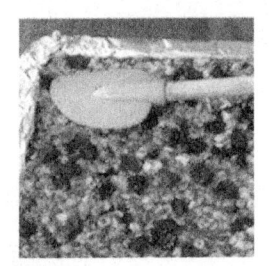

Cover the baking pan with aluminum foil and put it in the fridge for at least 2 hours (better overnight).

Remove the bars from the baking pan and cut into 12 even bars.

Store the healthy no-bake granola bars in an airtight container in the refrigerator for up to 2 weeks.

Enjoy!